THE LITTLE BOOK OF

MISQUOTATIONS

THE FAKEST *of* FAKE QUOTES, FALSE ATTRIBUTIONS, *and* FLAT-OUT LIES

Written by Lou Harry

WHALEN
BOOK · WORKS

Kennebunkport, Maine

For James Randi,
inspirational truth-seeker.

The Little Book of Misquotations

13-digit ISBN: 978-1-732-51262-7
10-digit ISBN: 1-732-51262-0

This book may be ordered by mail from the publisher. Please include $5.99 for postage and handling. Please support your local bookseller first

Books published by Whalen Book Works are available at special discounts when purchased in bulk. For more information, please email us at info@whalenbookworks.com.

Whalen Book Works
68 North Street
Kennebunkport, ME 04046

www.whalenbookworks.com

Cover and interior design by Melissa Gerber
Typography: Ball-Pen, Frente H1, Gotham, Kapra, Microbrew, ITC Caslon 224, Adobe Caslon Bodoni Poster, Bodoni, Fontbox Boathouse, and Festivo LC.

Printed in China
1 2 3 4 5 6 7 8 9 0

First Edition

CONTENTS

Introduction

You can quote me on this. In my first magazine job, a writer/editor on staff interviewed me for a story. Because my desk was right outside his office, I was an easy source to track down.

My circumstances fit neatly into a story he was writing, so I was a valid source. But since I worked with him, he thought it best to change my name. Fair enough. When I saw the story in print, though, I realized that he had also seen fit to change my quotes.

There wasn't much I could do at the time, given his seniority at the publication. But the incident planted in me a sensitivity to the misquote, whether deliberately altered or naively misstated.

As my journalism career continued, I developed a further appreciation for the challenge of accurate quoting. And as social media began to infiltrate society, I saw a greater and greater disregard for that accuracy.

In short, many people don't seem to care if they are getting a quote right or even attributing it to the right person.

I hope, by picking up this book, you aren't one of those people. You, good reader, care about truth. You want to know who said what and what was said by whom. You want to believe what you read. You want journalists—as well as your cousin on Facebook—to be able to back up what they write or post.

I trust you will let me know if I've made any mistakes.

—*Lou Harry*

Carl Sagan J. K. Rowling Confucius Jay
Audrey Hepburn C. S. Lewis Betty Whi
Ricky Gervais Charles Manson Bill Gates
Seuss P. T. Barnum Bill Murray Drake To
Brady Marilyn Monroe Barack Obama W.
B. Du Bois Mahatma Gandhi Keanu Reev
Alexandria Ocasio-Cortez Aristotle Jos
Stalin Donald Trump Dr. Martin Luth
King, Jr. Benjamin Franklin Outkast Glo
Steinem Banksy A. A. Milne Kurt Vonneg
Jr. George Carlin Susan B. Anthony Ben
Mussolini Meryl Streep The Bible Muhamm
Ali Taylor Swift Henry David Thore
George Washington Darth Vader Abraha
Lincoln William Tecumseh Sherman Fra
Zappa Mr. Spock (Leonard Nimoy) Elean
Roosevelt Gordon Gecko (Michael Dougla
Oprah Winfrey William Shakespeare Ku
Cobain Sun Tzu Maya Angelou Buddha E
Peron Isaac Newton Ann Richards Laur
Anderson Mike Pence Tarzan Ralph Wal
Emerson Steve Martin Ambrose Bier
Captain Kirk (William Shatner) Anne Ri
Franz Kafka Nelson Mandela Bob Dyl
Thomas Jefferson Kanye West Volta
Niccolò Machiavelli Rick Blaine (Humphr
Bogart) Barack Obama Thomas Edis
The Bhagavad Gita Harriet Tubman
Scott Fitzgerald Steve Jobs Jack Kerou

SOMEBODY ELSE SAID IT

Someone said it. Just not the person being given credit. Welcome to the fertile world of misattributions, a land where **Confucius** is confused with **Lao Tzu** and where **Marianne Williamson**'s words somehow get put into the mouth of **Nelson Mandela**.

"The journey of a thousand miles begins with a single step."

—*Confucius*

For some, it seems just as easy to assign this quote to Confucius, who lived and philosophized between 551 and 479 BC, as it is to give it to the person who actually said it, **Lao Tzu**, the father of Taoism. He was born in 601 BC, so there was some overlap—and legend has it that the two did actually meet. But not to share the same quote.

"For attractive lips, speak words of kindness."

—*Audrey Hepburn*

The source of this lovely bit of advice is actually humorist/essayist **Sam Levenson**, who included it in his book *In One Era and Out the Other*. So why does Audrey Hepburn get all the credit? Sean Hepburn Ferrer read passages from it at Hepburn's funeral, adding that his famous mother loved the text.

"Give a girl the right shoes and she'll conquer the world."

—Marilyn Monroe

It's easy for meme makers to put Monroe's name on just about any quote having to do with style. But this one was most likely said more than two decades after the cinematic icon's death by a music icon, **Bette Midler**, albeit with **"correct footwear"** instead of **"right shoes."**

"Wear sunscreen."

—*Kurt Vonnegut Jr.*

"What I said to **Mary Schmich** on the telephone was that what she wrote was funny and wise and charming, so I would have been proud had the words been mine." So said Kurt Vonnegut, who virally was given credit for a column written by *Chicago Tribune* scribe Mary Schmich, who was imagining what she would written were she asked to deliver a graduate speech. Her words, including the sunscreen advice, somehow transmogrified into a speech that Vonnegut allegedly gave at MIT. Never happened. But according to Vonnegut, even his wife, Jill Krementz, fell for it: When she received it via email, she, too, forwarded to friends and family.

"Rule No. 1: Life is not fair. Get used to it."

—*Bill Gates*

Not to be outdone by Vonnegut, Bill Gates also gets credit for a graduation speech he never gave. His involved a series of life lessons beginning with the one above and ending with **"Rule No. 11: Be nice to nerds. You may end up working for them. We all could."** For the rest of the list—and the true author, check out **Charles J. Sykes**'s *50 Rules Kids Won't Learn in School: Real-World Antidotes to Feel-Good Education*.

"Good girls go to heaven. Bad girls go everywhere."

—Helen Gurley Brown

Visit any honky-tonk boardwalk town and you are likely to find this one printed on a tight T-shirt. Search online and you'll see it credited not only to the feminist leader but also to **Bette Midler**, **Katherine Hepburn**, and **Mae West**. It's even the title of a 1994 **Meat Loaf** ballad (lyrics by Jim Steinman). While they all may have said it (or sang it) at one time or another, it's a variant on an old joke, going back nearly a century, original quipster unknown.

"Why do people say 'grow some balls'? Balls are weak and sensitive! If you really want to get tough, grow a vagina! Those things take a pounding!"

—*Betty White*

White said a lot of very funny things in her decades as a staple on TV sitcoms and game shows. But this isn't one of them. Snopes traced this one back to comedian **Sheng Wang** as well as a routine by comic **Hal Sparks**—both of whom, while funny, can only dream of having a career like White's.

"The Lord works in mysterious ways."
—*The Bible*

Perhaps. But this didn't get around to print until **William Cowper** included **"God moves in a mysterious way"** in a 1773 hymn.

"I'm the devil, and I'm here to do the devil's work."
—*Charles Manson*

While the warped mind behind the Tate-Labianca murders is sometimes cited as spouter of this—and the description fits— the words were actually spoken by **Charles "Tex" Watson**, a member of the Manson "family." He was found guilty on seven counts of first-degree murder.

"Life is what you do while you're waiting to die."

—*Donald Trump*

Yes, Donald Trump did make this nihilistic comment on multiple occasions. But the line actually should be attributed to **Fred Ebb**, the lyricist side of Kander and Ebb, the songwriting team responsible for such Broadway shows as *Cabaret* and *Chicago*. The line comes from a song in one of the duos' lesser-known shows, *Zorba*, based on the popular novel and film *Zorba the Greek*. (Trivia: In the revival of the musical, starring the film's star, Anthony Quinn, the line was tweaked to **"Life is what you do till the moment you die,"** making it ever-so-slightly less depressing.)

"Life is tough, but it's tougher when you're stupid."

—*John Wayne*

The Duke had a lot of memorable lines in movies, particularly in cinematic westerns. But this one wasn't one of them. Its source is the **George V. Higgins** 1971 novel *The Friends of Eddie Coyle*, which was made into a movie just a few years later. Both contain the line, **"This life's hard, man, but it's harder if you're stupid."**

"Music washes away the dust of everyday life."

—*Red Auerbach*

It's a lovely image. And concertgoers are likely to heartily agree with its sentiment. But regardless of what you may have read in a news story about the Emerson String Quartet or in a barbershop quartet newsletter (just two of the places where it's been misattributed), the quote was not said by Red Auerbach, the legendary Boston Celtics basketball coach. Who did say it? **Berthold Auerbach**, a nineteenth-century German poet and philosopher who was well read but not, well, Red.

"Whatever you can do or dream you can, begin it. Boldness has genius, power, and magic in it."

—*Johann Wolfgang von Goethe*

You've got a choice. You can trust an unknown poster on Goodreads. Or you can believe the researches at the Goethe Society of North America who searched for the source of the quote for two years and concluded that it doesn't belong to their literary hero but to **William Hutchinson Murray**, author of *The Scottish Himalayan Expedition*. That didn't keep Goethe from getting credit for the line in *The San Francisco Chronicle*.

"Skate to where the puck is going, not to where it is."

—*Wayne Gretzsky*

Fast Company tracked this one down and found out that it wasn't said by the hockey great—but by his father, **Walter Gretzsky**. He clarified to the reporter that the quote is actually, **"Go to where the puck is going, not where it has been,"** and admitted that the advice is meant **"strictly for little kids."**

"Those who stand for nothing fall for anything."

—*Alexander Hamilton*

Why credit the Founding Father (and not yet Broadway leading player) with this quote? Perhaps that's because it was uttered by British broadcaster **Alex Hamilton**. It's also been attributed to actress **Irene Dunne** and others. The original source, though, is unknown.

"To sin by silence when they should protest makes cowards of men."

—*Abraham Lincoln*

It's a noble idea, yes. But it's a noble idea that came not from Honest Abe, but from prolific American writer **Ella Wheeler Wilcox**. It's from her poem "An Ambitious Man." Blame General Douglas MacArthur, who credited Lincoln with the line during a speech in 1950.

"I will not follow where the path may lead, but I will go where there is no path, and I will leave a trail."

—*Ralph Waldo Emerson*

It's not just social media that screws up credit for quotes. Academic journals can, too. And their credibility can lead to a rabbit hole of misinformation. *Middle School Journal* is the publication that linked it to Emerson in 1992. The lines actually do come from a poem, just not one by him. They are in "Wind-Wafted Wild Flowers" by **Muriel Strode**, published in 1903.

"**Our deepest fear is not that we are inadequate. Our deepest fear is that we are powerful beyond measure. It is our light, not our darkness, that most frightens us. We ask ourselves, 'Who am I to be brilliant, gorgeous, talented, and fabulous?' Actually, who are you not to be? You are a child of God. Your playing small does not serve the world.**"

—*Nelson Mandela*

You can find many options for purchasing inspirational posters of this quote. Just know that it isn't Mandela who said it but self-help bestselling author **Marianne Williamson**. While you can't find it in any Mandela speech, you can find it in Williamson's Book *A Return to Love*.

> **"Don't bend; don't water it down, don't try to make it logical; don't edit your own soul according to the fashion. Rather, follow your most intense obsessions mercilessly."**

—*Franz Kafka*

Here's a case where a writer—**Anne Rice**—was trying to describe the philosophy of another writer, Franz Kafka. The words quoted above come from her forward to a collection of his short stories and were later misattributed to Kafka himself. Rice chimed in via a 2015 Facebook post: **"Those are my words struggling to define the impression Kafka's example made on me! And it's being attributed worldwide to Kafka. What a shame. I think Kafka might have expressed those sentiments a lot better!"**

"An election is a sort of advance auction sale of stolen goods."

—Ambrose Bierce

Nope. It was **H. L. Mencken** in his essay "Sham Battle," published in *The Baltimore Evening Sun*. He wrote: **"In other words, government is a broker in pillage, and every election is a sort of advance auction sale of stolen goods."**

"A system cannot fail those it was never built to protect."

—*W. E. B. Du Bois*

According to *Time* magazine, **Rihanna** may be the unintentional root of the confusion surrounding this quote. Following the acquittal of George Zimmerman in the killing of Trayvon Martin, she tweeted the quote without any attribution. Then it started to appear in multiple online stories, somehow acquiring historian Du Bois as its dubious source. *Time* dug further and found that the actual source was *The Atlantic* journalist **Vann R. Newkirk II**, who tweeted it under what was his joke handle at the time, **W.E.B.B.I.E. Du Bois**.

"Pressure is something you feel when you don't know what you're doing."

—*Peyton Manning*

It's a noble quote that seems in line with the philosophy of one of the leading quarterbacks of all time. But contrary to what you might read on multiple websites, lazily researched "my hero" school term papers, and the wall of a burger joint in Central Indiana, Manning didn't originate the pithy saying. He was, in fact, quoting Pittsburgh Steelers coach **Chuck Noll**.

"It's not the size of the dog in the fight. It's the size of the fight in the dog."

—Michael Vick

Sometimes, the pairing of a quote and its nonauthor is meant to be funny. But then it takes on a life of its own from those who don't get the joke. In this case, the quote decidedly didn't come from the football player who made headlines for animal abuse. It's also often credited to **Mark Twain**, who didn't say it either.

"Writing about music is like dancing about architecture."

—Elvis Costello

No, it wasn't Costello. Or **Frank Zappa**. Or **Laurie Anderson**. Or **Steve Martin**. The most likely candidate in a crowded field? Comic actor **Martin Mull**.

"Music hath charms to soothe the savage beast."

—William Shakespeare

There are two problems here. The first is that the quote comes from **William Congreve**, who kicks off his 1697 play *The Mourning Bride* with it, not from Shakespeare. The second is that it's "breast," not "beast." The full line from the tragedy: "Musick has Charms to sooth a savage Breast, / To soften Rocks, or bend a knotted Oak."

"Whenever I hear the word culture, I reach for my pistol."

—*Hermann Goering*

Nein. The quote actually, with a small change, comes from **Hanns Johst**'s 1933 play *Schlageter*. The play concerns Albert Leo Schlageter, the real-life German saboteur who was court martialed by the French and executed.

"None of us are getting out of here alive, so please stop treating yourself like an afterthought."

—*Richard Gere*

She may not have the box-office clout of Richard Gere—or **Anthony Hopkins**, who is often given credit as well—but the quote came from **Nanea Hoffman**, who wrote it on the java-fueled Facebook page of Sweatpants & Coffee. She commented later that she found the misattributions **"weirdly flattering."**

"The only two certainties in life are death and taxes."

—*Mark Twain*

It is unclear whether **Edward Ward** or **Christopher Bullock** came up with this popular phrase, but one thing's for sure—it wasn't Mark Twain who said it first. Like Gandhi and Marilyn Monroe, Mark Twain was so prolific, he gets credit for loads of other people's work.

"Be who you are and say what you feel because those who mind don't matter, and those who matter don't mind."

—*Dr. Seuss*

An elephant may be faithful 100 percent, as the good doctor said, but memories of humans aren't always 100 percent accurate. In this case, in spite of what you may have read online, Dr. Seuss doesn't deserve credit for this one. Who does? That could be either **Sir Mark Young** in a 1945 issue of *Insurance Newsweek* or **Bernard Baruch**, responding to a columnist in the New York *Journal-American*.

"To avoid criticism, say nothing, do nothing, and be nothing."

—*Aristotle*

Even *Forbes* magazine bought into the idea that the Greek philosopher warned that nothing gets done by taking the quiet road. However, the quote actually comes from the lesser-known philosopher (and travelling salesman) **Elbert Hubbard** in a book about automotive pioneer John North Willys.

"There's a sucker born every minute."

—*P. T. Barnum*

With the image makeover granted him by the positive portrayal in the musical movie *The Greatest Showman*, this might be a good time to clear up the origin of P. T. Barnum's most quoted phrase. If only it were that easy.

The phrase and its variants have been used by gamblers and confidence men to denigrate their marks, but there's no evidence that the circus-owning king of the hucksters said anything like it. It was Barnum's rival—and occasional partner, **Adam Forepaugh**, who credited P. T. with the pithy quote.

Who actually said it? That's still a subject of debate, with con man **Joseph Bessimer** and Chicago saloon owner **Michael Cassius McDonald** being among the front-runners.

"Better to remain silent and be thought of a fool than to speak and remove all doubt."

—*Abraham Lincoln*

Of course, this quote seems like something that might have been said by the sixteenth president, who actually did say **"If I were two faced, would I be wearing this one?"** and many other justifiably famed quips. But, alas, it's just another piece of Abe Apocrypha.

It wasn't attributed to Lincoln until it appeared in a 1931 magazine—more than two decades after it first showed up by its likely author, **Maurice Switzer**, who may in turn have been inspired by the Bible quote: **"Even a fool, when he holdeth his peace, is counted wise: and he that shutteth his lips is esteemed a man of understanding."**

"Standing on the shoulders of giants."

—Isaac Newton

Yes, he said it, and the fuller quote is, **"If I have seen a little further it is by standing on the shoulders of giants."** But he wasn't the first to use that metaphor. **John of Salisbury**, in his 1159 treatise *Metalogicon* said, **"We are like dwarfs sitting on the shoulders of giants."** And he may have picked it up from French philosopher **Bernard of Chartres**. Since then, it's been borrowed by **Samuel Coleridge**, **Stephen Hawking**, and a parade of politicians from **Disraeli** to **Reagan**.

"He was born on third base and thought he hit a triple."

—*Ann Richards*

Texas governor Richards did take digs at George Bush at the 1988 Democratic National Convention—including claiming he was **"born with a silver foot in his mouth."** But although this quote is often attributed to her, it was a day later when columnist **Jim Hightower** added, **"His is an upper class world in which wealth is given to you at birth. He is a man who was born on third base and thinks he hit a triple."** Actor **Martin Sheen** later used the same phrase to describe **Mitt Romney**—although Sheen at least referred to it as an "old phrase." Even so, football coach **Barry Switzer** seems to have beaten all of them to the punch line saying, in a 1986 *Chicago Tribune* story, **"Some people are born on third base and go through life thinking they hit a triple."**

"The price of liberty is eternal vigilance."

—Thomas Jefferson

Not only was it not Jefferson who said this, it was not **Frederick Douglass**, **James Buchanan**, or **William Henry Harrison**, as is often said. A slightly longer version has been traced to Irish politician **John Philpot Curran**.

"I know why the caged bird sings."

—*Maya Angelou*

There's no denying that she wrote the book. And a poem of the same name. But the words originated in another poem, by **Paul Laurence Dunbar** titled "Sympathy." Dunbar's lines: **"I know why the caged bird sings, ah me, / When his wing is bruised and his bosom sore, / When he beats his bars and would be free."**

"Holding onto anger is like grasping a hot coal and hoping someone else will get burned."

—Buddha

Close. This quote is a popular rephrasing of the words of **Buddhagho**, a fifth-century scholar, interpreting the words of Buddha.

"Keep your friends close, and your enemies closer."

—*Sun Tzu*

Although Sun Tzu and **Niccolò Machiavelli** (who is also sometimes credited) had similar ideas, the quote actually comes from a great sage known as, wait for it, *The Godfather Part II*.

"Your worth consists in what you are and not in what you have. What you are will show in what you do."

—*Thomas Edison*

So, he wasn't a prolific inventor like Edison. But the man who actually wrote these words, **Thomas Davidson**, did pen such books as *The Philosophical System of Antonio Rosmini-Serbati*, *Rousseau and Education According to Nature*, and the source of this quote: *The Education of Wage-Earners*.

"Trying to be happy by accumulating possessions is like trying to satisfy hunger by taping sandwiches all over your body."

—*George Carlin*

It's safe to say that **Roger J. Corless**, author of *Vision of Buddhism: The Space Under the Tree*, never gets credit for George Carlin's classic comedy routine "Seven Dirty Words You Can't Say on Television." Yet Carlin keeps getting credit for these lines by the late Duke University professor of religion.

"If it can be destroyed by the truth, it deserves to be destroyed by the truth."

—*Carl Sagan*

While the scientist and TV personality was a steadfast seeker of the truth, he wasn't the person who originated this quote. That was actually science fiction writer **P. C. Hodgell** who, in her novel *Seeker's Mask*, wrote **"That which can be destroyed by the truth, should be."** It wasn't until nine years later that the altered statement began showing up online credited to Sagan.

"I will return, and I will be millions."

—*Eva Peron*

Although a variation on those words do appear on the grave of the former first lady of Argentina, they weren't added there until a decade after her death and were taken from a poem by **José María Casiñeira de Dios** writing in Peron's voice. Clouding the matter further, the words were also featured in **Howard Fast**'s novel *Spartacus* (and in **Stanley Kubrick**'s film version) and have been traced back to the poet **Tupac Katari**, who said similar words before his execution in 1781.

"Great things are not accomplished by those who yield to trends and fads and popular opinion."

—Jack Kerouac

Or so wrote a columnist for the *Marin Independent Journal* and a reporter for *Forbes*. Perhaps it's understandable—but not excusable—that a quote that actually came from **Charles Kuralt**, the face of the CBS Evening News segment "On the Road" could be mistaken for one by the author of *On the Road*. It's just surprising that it hasn't also been credited to **Willie Nelson**, who sang "On the Road Again."

"Cooking is like love. It should be entered into with abandon or not at all."

—*Julia Child*

No matter what it says on the apron you got for your aunt on Etsy, Child didn't say it. The quote comes from pioneer radio and TV critic **Helen van Horne**.

"I no longer have patience for certain things, not because I've become arrogant, but simply because I reached a point in my life where I do not want to waste more time with what displeases me or hurts me."

— *Meryl Streep*

Such was the opening of a lengthy bit of self-help offered, allegedly, by the acclaimed actress—who never claimed to say anything like this. In fact, it was self-help author **José Micard Teixeira**, who tried in vain to set the record straight when the quote started appearing. According to Senior Planet, the quote—credited to Streep—was first posted by a Romanian blogger. Its viral path included shares from the likes of singers **Janis Ian** and **Julian Lennon**.

"To laugh often and much; to win the respect of intelligent people and the affection of children; to leave the world a better place; to know even one life has breathed easier because you have lived. This is to have succeeded."

—*Ralph Waldo Emerson*

Pity **Bessie Anderson Stanley**. She entered a contest that asked for an answer to the question, **"What constitutes success?"** According to *Forbes* magazine, she won $250 for her efforts. Unfortunately, a syndicated columnist attributed her lines to the famed poet. And then yet another columnist, **Ann Landers**, duplicated the same mistake. Twice.

"Don't fire till you see the whites of their eyes."

—*Andrew Jackson*

Accuracy is usually assisted by proximity when it comes to the use of firearms. But although Andrew Jackson is often credited with this statement in relation to the Battle of New Orleans during (or, in some views, after) the War of 1812, it goes further back to the American Revolution. Who said it? Some claim **General Israel Putnam**. Others say **Colonel William Prescott**. The phrase may also go back further—and overseas—to **Prince Charles of Prussia**. Unfortunately, one of the first sources is the wildly unreliable historian **Mason Weems**, who is also the source of the George Washington cherry tree chopping myth.

"Dissent is the highest form of patriotism."

—*Thomas Jefferson*

Popularized by John Lindsay, mayor of New York City, during the Columbia University protests of the Vietnam War, the quote—often sourced to Thomas Jefferson—actually only goes back to 1961, according to the folks at Monticello. The earliest source is a booklet, "The Use of Force in International Affairs," and it was phrased in the form of a question: **"If what your country is doing seems to you practically and morally wrong, is dissent the highest form of patriotism?"**

"Some people feel the rain. Others just get wet."

—Bob Marley

The great reggae singer didn't say it. Neither did **Shakespeare**, as some have claimed. Most likely, it was a more playful character, singer and songwriter **Roger Miller**, best known for his countrified hits "Dang Me" and "King of the Road."

"I may be drunk, Bessie, but you are ugly, and tomorrow I shall be sober."

—*Winston Churchill*

According to Richard M. Langworth at WinstonChurchill.org, the prime minister did, in fact, share words to that effect with fellow politician Bessie Braddock. Langworth said the story was told to him by Churchill's bodyguard, so perhaps there should be some allowance for whisper-down-the-lane alterations. But even if he did say it, the words probably didn't originate with Churchill. In the popular 1934 movie *It's a Gift*, a drunk **Harold Bissonette (played by W. C. Fields)** responds to accusations that he is drunk by saying, **"Yeah, and you're crazy. But I'll be sober tomorrow and you'll be crazy the rest of your life."** Screenplay credit, by the way, goes to **Jack Cunningham**, although others also contributed to the final script.

"England and America are two countries divided by a common language."

—*George Bernard Shaw*

While he liked to write about language (see his play *Pygmalion* among others), Shaw shouldn't be given credit for this one. It is similar, though, to **Oscar Wilde**'s line in *The Canterville Ghost*, **"We really have everything in common with America nowadays except, of course, language."**

"Americans can always be counted on to do the right thing, after they've tried everything else."

—*Winston Churchill*

Oooh, snap. The British prime minister takes a shot at that big country across the sea. Problem is, the quote—at least, variations on it—was actually first uttered by Israeli diplomat **Abba Eban** and he referred to **"men and nations,"** not strictly **"Americans."**

"The secret of change is to focus all of your energy, not on fighting the old, but on building the new."

—*Socrates*

So went the quote tweeted by **Ivanka Trump**. Well, she was almost right. The quote actually comes from a book called *Way of the Peaceful Warrior: A Book That Changes Lives* by gymnast **Dan Millman**. The fictional memoir puts those words in the mouth of a gas station attendant who helps the main character find enlightenment. That wisdom-spouting pumper's name? Socrates. (The president's daughter later deleted and reposted a correction for her tweet.)

"If I had more time, I would have written a shorter letter."

—*Mark Twain*

Do great minds truly think alike? You'd have to believe that to buy the idea that **John Locke**, **Benjamin Franklin**, **Woodrow Wilson**, **Henry David Thoreau**, and Mark Twain all independently came up with variations on this phrase. While there's documentation for all but Twain for similar quotes, the root most likely is French mathematician **Blaise Pascal** who wrote, in the original French, ***"Je n'ai fait celle-ci plus longue que parce que je n'ai pas eu le loisir de la faire plus courte."***

"We are what we repeatedly do. Excellence, then, is not an act, but a habit."

—*Aristotle*

Just because a Patriot—in this case, retiring New England Patriot **Matt Light**—gave credit to Aristotle, doesn't mean the great teacher actually said or wrote this bit of stick-to-itiveness wisdom. The source is the lower profile **Will Durant**, who summarized Aristotle in *The Story of Philosophy: The Lives and Opinions of the World's Greatest Philosophers*.

Carl Sagan J. K. Rowling Confucius Jay
Audrey Hepburn C. S. Lewis Betty Wh
Ricky Gervais Charles Manson Bill Gates
Seuss P. T. Barnum Bill Murray Drake To
Brady Marilyn Monroe Barack Obama W.
B. Du Bois Mahatma Gandhi Keanu Reev
Alexandria Ocasio-Cortez Aristotle Jos
Stalin Donald Trump Dr. Martin Luth
King, Jr. Benjamin Franklin Outkast Glo
Steinem Banksy A. A. Milne Kurt Vonneg
Jr. George Carlin Susan B. Anthony Ben
Mussolini Meryl Streep The Bible Muhamm
Ali Taylor Swift Henry David Thore
George Washington Darth Vader Abrah
Lincoln William Tecumseh Sherman Fra
Zappa Mr. Spock (Leonard Nimoy) Elean
Roosevelt Gordon Gecko (Michael Dougla
Oprah Winfrey William Shakespeare K
Cobain Sun Tzu Maya Angelou Buddha E
Peron Isaac Newton Ann Richards Lau
Anderson Mike Pence Tarzan Ralph Wal
Emerson Steve Martin Ambrose Bie
Captain Kirk (William Shatner) Anne Ri
Franz Kafka Nelson Mandela Bob Dyl
Thomas Jefferson Kanye West Volta
Niccolo Machiavelli Rick Blaine (Humphr
Bogart) Barack Obama Thomas Edis
The Bhagavad Gita Harriet Tubman
Scott Fitzgerald Steve Jobs Jack Kero

NOBODY SAID IT

If you are going to quote someone, quote a real person and quote them accurately. To paraphrase someone who isn't **Voltaire** (see page 102), not only do I disapprove of what you say, but I won't defend your right to say it.

"I want to suck your blood."

—Dracula

Despite the notorious vampire's well-documented taste for plasma and platelets, the reality is that the count himself never uttered this oft-quoted phrase. Not in **Bram Stoker**'s original novel or in **Bela Lugosi**'s famed staged and screen performances, anyway. The closest line in the original film is actually a bit wittier: when offered an adult beverage, Count Dracula replies, **"I never drink...wine."**

"Let them eat cake!"

—Marie Antoinette

Callousness doesn't get much more concise than in this quote, commonly attributed to the wife of France's King Louis XVI. So hated was she that she would find herself in a guillotine not long after the revolution began.

Like many an urban myth, though, the story had been making the rounds before Marie Antoinette was said to have said it. French philosopher **Jean-Jacques Rousseau** included the anecdote in referencing "a great princess," thought to be Marie-Therese.

For the record, he/she didn't mention cake at all—it was brioche.

"First they ignore you. Then they laugh at you. Then they attack you. Then you win."

—*Mahatma Gandhi*

An inspirational quote often offered with Gandhi's name attached, this one doesn't have a clear actual source— although *The Christian Science Monitor* found it strikingly similar to one used by **Nicholas Klein** in a 1918 talk to the Amalgamated Clothing Workers of America.

"It's déjà vu all over again!"

—Yogi Berra

Yogi Berra's reputation as a baseball player and coach is only equaled by his reputation as the coiner of less-than-logical phrases. For instance, he did say, "When you come to a fork in the road, take it" to a graduating class in 1996. But as to the déjà vu quote, Berra informed William Safire, writing for *The New York Times*, "Nope, not true, I never said that." And that was backed up by Quote Investigator, which tracked down "It's déjà vu again" to a 1962 poem by Jim Prior in a Florida newspaper. Keep in mind. Berra later backpedaled and took credit for the line. But keep in mind that this is the same person who said, **"I never said most of the things I said."**

"Here's to the crazy ones. The misfits. The rebels. The troublemakers. The round pegs in the square holes. The ones who see things differently. They're not fond of rules, and they have no respect for the status quo. You can quote them; disagree with them; glorify or vilify them. About the only thing you can't do is ignore them. Because they change things."

—Jack Kerouac

No, it's not a missing chapter from *On the Road*. It's actually just text from **an Apple marketing campaign**.

"A man needs truth like a machine needs oil."

—*Jack Kerouac*

No, he didn't say this one, either. But actor **Jean-Marc Barr playing Jack Kerouac** did...in the movie ***Big Sur***.

"I freed a thousand slaves. I could have freed over a thousand more if they knew they were slaves."

—*Harriet Tubman*

The quote may be accurate numerically. But no one has been able to track down a trustworthy source for the actual quote. Snopes traced it to an essay by **Robin Morgan**, noting that some historians find the apocryphal quote trivializes the enormous forces acting against those in servitude, implying that there was "tacit consent."

"Well behaved women rarely make history."

—*Marilyn Monroe*

Bumper stickers would have you believe otherwise, but those words were in fact written by an American historian of early America and the history of women at Harvard, professor **Laurel Thatcher Ulrich**, while she was a student at the University of New Hampshire. No one knows why the most popular mid-century movie star gets all the credit.

"I cannot tell a lie."

—*George Washington*

The story goes that a six-year-old G. W. was gifted a hatchet as a gift and took it to one of his family's trees. When questioned by his angry papa, he allegedly recited this oft-repeated line and his honesty was celebrated. According to the folks at the Mount Vernon historical site, however, the myth was created by **Mason Locke Weems**, one of the first POTUS's first biographers. The story first appeared in the fifth edition of his *The Life of Washington*, published in 1806.

"Strategery."

—*George W. Bush*

"You have to admit that in my sentences I go where no man has gone before." So said (for real) President George W. Bush at the White House correspondents' dinner, mocking his penchant for malaprops. "Our enemies are innovative and resourceful, and so are we," he once said, which would have been fine if he didn't add: "They never stop thinking about new ways to harm our country and our people, and neither do we." But the slip of the tongue he's most known for—the use of the nonword "strategery," actually comes from the tongue of comedian **Will Ferrell**, playing the POTUS in a 2000 *SNL* sketch.

"The ends justify the means."

—*Niccolò Machiavelli*

The Florentine political philosopher—most famous for writing *The Prince*—has become the go-to guy for referencing tyrannical power. But scholars disagree on his intent—while being clear that he isn't responsible for this end-game rationalization of morally questionable behavior. He did offer the slightly less aggressive quote: **"That which is good for the enemy harms you, and that which is good for you harms the enemy."**

"Stop asking me to explain."

—*Bob Dylan*

Fair to say that Dylan hasn't been into explaining his songs. But *New Yorker* writer **Jonah Lehrer** made up that and many other quotes from the troubadour to flesh out his book, *Imagine: How Creativity Works*. Word didn't get out until the 2012 book was already rising on Amazon's rankings. Publisher Houghton Mifflin promptly withdrew the title.

"Today I have 18 Academy Awards."

—*Meryl Streep*

Over a million likes and a few hundred thousand shares don't make something true. In this case, a photo of a youthful Streep on the subway was accompanied by a lengthy quote that read: **"This was me on my way home from an audition for King Kong where I was told I was too 'ugly' for the part. This was a pivotal moment for me. This one rogue opinion could derail my dreams of becoming an actress or force me to pull myself up by the bootstraps and believe in myself. I took a deep breath and said, 'I'm sorry you think I'm too ugly for your film but you're just one opinion in a sea of thousands and I'm off to find a kinder tide. Today I have 18 Academy Awards.'"** Inspiring, yes. And she did appear on *The Graham Norton Show* telling the story of being rejected from *King Kong*. But the quote was made and paired with the photo on a now-deleted fan page.

"My job's as hard as fighting in Afghanistan."

—*Tom Cruise*

Are actors that out of it? Some websites would like us to believe that. But what Cruise actually said was far milder. While giving a deposition for a lawsuit against magazines claiming he abandoned his child, he was asked about the prolonged periods on movie sets leading to absence from family—something his lawyer had equated with serving in the Afghanistan. Cruise responded: **"I didn't hear the Afghanistan [comment], but that's what it feels like, and certainly on this last movie, it was brutal. It was brutal."** What TMZ and others failed to note is the follow-up, in which the lawyer asked, "Do you believe the situations are the same?"—and Cruise replied, **"Oh, come on!"**

"If I can't dance to it, it's not my revolution."

—*Emma Goldman*

The noted anarchist did say in her autobiography, "At the dances I was one of the most untiring and gayest." And after being told by a fellow traveler that her frivolity would hurt the causes she was fighting for, she blew off the guy, later writing, **"I did not believe that a Cause which stood for a beautiful ideal, for anarchism, for release and freedom from conventions and prejudice, should demand the denial of life and joy."** Unfortunately, that doesn't fit as easily on a coffee mug as this pithy quote, which appeared in, among other places, The Daily Beast.

"I don't know, ask Prince."

—*Eric Clapton*

That's the response the musician on the short list of greatest guitar players in the world allegedly said when asked what it was like to be the greatest guitar player in the world. The reality, though, is that Clapton never said it and the same story was floated decades earlier, only that time it was **Jimi Hendrix** being asked and his answer: **Phil Keaggy**.

"I can see Russia from my house."

—*Sarah Palin*

The would-be United States vice president did say, in an interview with ABC News, that **"you can actually see Russia from land here in Alaska, from an island in Alaska."** But it took the writers at *SNL* to put a funnier version of those words into the mouth of **Tina Fey** in one of many appearances as Palin.

"**I was recently on a tour of Latin America, and the only regret I have was that I didn't study Latin harder in school so I could converse with those people.**"

—*Dan Quayle*

For eight or so years, mocking Vice President Dan Quayle seemed to be a national pastime. Not only did people repeat his flubs, they created ones that could have been his. Such was the case with this quote, which was shared by Rhode Island Representative **Claudine Schneider**—who concluded by saying it was a joke. That didn't keep it from being shared as truth in multiple news outlets.

"The British are coming! The British are coming!"

—*Paul Revere*

Although his urgent journey achieved legendary status thanks to the poem by **Henry Wadsworth Longfellow**, Paul Revere is unlikely to have shouted anything in his efforts—along with two fellow riders—to warn that the redcoats were on their way. **More likely, his warnings were quiet, given the need to keep the knowledge secret.** Revere was also captured, but that's a longer story.

"I will not die until America is destroyed."

—*Fidel Castro*

The proximity of Castro's death to the election of **Donald Trump** as President of the United States led to this meme. The joke might have been funnier if Castro had, in fact, made that statement.

"In the end I believe my generation will surprise everyone. We already know that both political parties are playing both sides from the middle and we'll elect a true outsider when we fully mature. I wouldn't be surprised if it's a business tycoon who can't be bought and who does what's right for the people. Someone like Donald Trump, as crazy as that sounds."

—*Kurt Cobain*

No, the Nirvana leader didn't predict the rise of Trump. But the naive—and those looking for counterculture support for their hero—somehow accepted the quote paired with Cobain's photo as fact. The misspelling of **Kurt** as **Curt** in the original posting should have been a tip-off.

"The only thing Negroes can do for me is buy my records and shine my shoes."

—*Elvis Presley*

The nasty rumor of this quote circulated in the 1957 leading *Jet* magazine to send a reporter to ask Elvis himself if he had said it. His response: **"I never said anything like that, and people who know me know I wouldn't have said it."** Further research from Snopes found the origin of the quote in a story about Elvis that quoted anonymous "people on the street" rather than the singer himself.

"You dirty rat."

—James Cagney

He came closest, perhaps, in the lesser known flick *Taxi* from 1932 in which he threatened a man in hiding with the colorful, "Come out and take it, ya dirty yellow-bellied rat...." But Cagney himself stated that the catch-phrase associated with him wasn't actually his. In accepting a lifetime achievement award from the American Film Institute, Cagney said to impressionist Frank Gorshin, **"Just in passing, I never said, 'You dirty rat,'"** What I actually did say was **'Judy, Judy, Judy.'"**

"Judy, Judy, Judy."

—*Cary Grant*

The acclaimed actor was notorious for never giving interviews. But at an audience Q&A, he was asked "Who is 'Judy, Judy, Judy'?"—referring to a phrase that celebrity impersonators frequently used to capture his distinct vocal style. His answer: **"As far as we know, we looked up track after track and outtake after outtake and I never said, 'Judy, Judy, Judy.' And we think it started with a fella called Larry Storch...who did imitations in those days."**

"You cannot find peace by avoiding life."

—*Virginia Woolf*

And, in this case, you cannot find the truth by avoiding a little research. In this case, the quote comes from the book and the film ***The Hours***, which is about, yes, Virginia Woolf.

"Most folks are about as happy as they make up their minds to be."

—*Abraham Lincoln*

Make an observation and people might agree or disagree with you. Make an observation and attribute it to a great leader and the reaction may tip more toward the former than the latter. That's the case with this dubious bit of folksy wisdom. In the 1960s positive-thinking touchstone movie ***Pollyanna***, it's attributed to Abe and the blame for that may fall on columnist Dr. Frank Crane, who cited it in a Syracuse newspaper column. There's no evidence of Lincoln or anyone else saying it before then.

"I believe
in pink...."

—Audrey Hepburn

It's available on paperweights and posters, but there's not any evidence that Audrey Hepburn listed any of the "beliefs" proposed in the lineup that begins with **"I believe in pink."** (Others include **"I believe that the happy girls are the prettiest girls."**) According to Wikiquote, there's no sign of it in print before 2008—fifteen years after the actress's death.

"I hate the word *homophobia.* It's not a phobia. You are not scared; you are an asshole."

—*Morgan Freeman*

Another example of "If people don't listen to you, create a parody Twitter account." Here, the writer of the quip included it under the Twitter handle **Tweets from God**, which included a photo of Freeman (who, side note, narrated the documentary series *The Story of God*).

"The secret to getting ahead is getting started."

—*Mark Twain*

Here's another one that seems to have attracted Twain's name without any hint of a source. When *Forbes* checked up on it, a representative at the Mark Twain House and Museum effectively shot it down. In the same story, though, the private company **Agatha Christie Limited** claimed authorship for the prolific mystery writer. That, however, hasn't been verified.

"You furnish the pictures, I'll furnish the war."

—*William Randolph Hearst*

In spite of it being quoted in *Politico* and many other respected outlets, it was never said, according to historian W. Joseph Campbell, author of the book *Getting It Wrong*. The alleged telegram to artist Frederic Remington, then a Hearst newspaper correspondent in Havana, would have been wildly reckless, noted Campbell, adding that there's no reliable documentation to back it up. He called it **"one of the most tenacious of all media myths."**

"I Spent all morning taking out a comma and all afternoon putting it back."

—*Gustave Flaubert*

When obsessive writers are discussed, this quote is likely to rear its head. And it's likely to be miscredited. There's no sign that Flaubert actually said it, alas, but there's a better than average chance that it's a condensed version of a story from **Oscar Wilde**.

"Me Tarzan, You Jane."

—Tarzan

You quote. You wrong. Not only didn't the jungle resident say this in any of the many iterations of *Tarzan* on film, he didn't say it in any of Edgar Rice Burroughs's novels either. There is a documented moment, however, of it being said by **Lupe Valez**, Mexican-born ex-wife of *Tarzan* screen star **Johnny Weissmuller**. When asked about her English proficiency, she reportedly said, **"I was married to a guy who can only say, 'Me Tarzan. You Jane.'"**

"Come with me to the Casbah."

—*Pépé le Moko*

Being mimicked by a celebrity impressionist is one thing. Having your accent and style adapted into a cartoon character is quite another. Thanks to Warner Bros. Cartoons **Pepé Le Pew** and **Bugs Bunny**, it became tough to take French actor **Charles Boyer** (who played gangster Pépé le Moko) very seriously. To add insult to mockery, the most famous line associated with Boyer—allegedly from the movie *Algiers*—wasn't even in the film.

"It is never too late to be what you might have been."

—*George Eliot*

You can't trust Goodreads. Or, apparently, self-helpers **Marianne Williamson** and **Tom Peters**. Those are just some of the sources claiming this to be a quote from the famed writer. But Rebecca Mead, writing in *The New Yorker*, said she could not find it anywhere in Eliot's letters or fiction. Neither had Eliot biographers.

"Obsess about your next customer, not only the ones you have."

—*J. K. Rowling*

Known primarily as a creator of magical worlds and not as a business consultant, Rowling was surprised to see on Twitter that motivational speaker Jeremy Gutsch had shared these words—along with a picture of her—as part of a presentation to a gathering of the Outdoor Industry Association. She tweeted back, "I have never said that in my life. Never. I don't have customers, I have readers. Why am I on that screen?" The OIA responded with "Our sincere apologies, we were covering a keynote presentation—the mischief has been managed (aka quickly deleted)!" but Gutsch kept up the engagement, tweeting back, "Not listed as a quote, but my lesson from your life story. DM me and I will send you the tale of how u inspired me." Rowling was skeptical. **"The meaning of my life is 'focus on new customers'? Wow...that's...not how it looks from the inside."**

"God made beer because he loves us and wants us to be happy."

—*Benjamin Franklin*

Trust the folks at the Franklin Institute in Franklin's old stomping grounds of Philadelphia. They say that the quote often found on brewpub t-shirts is a mangling of Franklin's actual comments about another adult beverage. In a circa-1779 letter, he wrote: **"Behold the rain which descends from heaven upon our vineyards; there it enters the roots of the vines, to be changed into wine; a constant proof that God loves us and loves to see us happy."**

"President Trump got all our favorite foods. It was the best meal we ever had."

—*Trevor Lawrence*

The meal in question—a selection of fast food offerings—got a lot of media attention when President Donald Trump served it to the NCAA champion Clemson football team at the White House. But although Clemson quarterback Trevor Lawrence did say that the trip to Washington was **"awesome,"** he publicly announced that the lengthier praise making the social media rounds was a fabrication.

"I'm the new King of Pop."

—*Kanye West*

Even though it was hatched on an allegedly comedic website, the naive on the internet—including some media outlets—picked up on this quote, allegedly uttered by West upon the death of Michael Jackson. When he got wind of the hoax, West turned to his blog, writing (for real): **"I have a feeling that this won't be the last false statement with my name on it, but this will be the last time I defend myself. I'm done."**

"Be yourself. Everyone else is already taken."

—Oscar Wilde

Wilde did say, **"One's real life is so often the life that one does not lead."** And he had a character in his novel *The Picture of Dorian Gray* say, **"Being natural is simply a pose."** But Quote Investigator and others could not find any Wildian source for this one, nor another credible possibility.

"It is impossible to rightly govern a nation without God and the Bible."

—*George Washington*

The quote may be a twist on this one: **"It is impossible to govern the universe without the aid of a Supreme Being,"** a statement attributed to Washington in an 1835 biography. But historians, including those at Mount Vernon, have not been able to source either of these quotations to the Founding Father himself—no matter how many people, including **Glenn Beck** and Iowa senator **Chuck Grassley**—want to use them as a justification to blur the line between religion and the state.

"If we don't do something about this president, I will."

—Barack Obama

No, the former President of the United States didn't say this about his successor at a Democratic National Committee fundraiser—in spite of statements reposted by conservative radio hosts saying he did. At that speech, he did say, **"This is a moment of great urgency and you are right to be concerned."**

"I disapprove of what you say, but I will defend to the death your right to say it."

—Voltaire

Sometimes biographical comment and condensation turns into misattribution or misquote. In this case, **Evelyn Beatrice Hall**, writing under the pseudonym **S. G. Tallentyre**, included the **"I disapprove of what you say..."** phrase in the book *The Friends of Voltaire*, published twenty-eight years after the famed author's death. But Hall/Tallentyre didn't actually quote Voltaire. She used the phrase to indicate Voltaire's attitude toward the burning of a book by philosopher **Claude-Adrien Helvetius**. Later, she made clear in a letter that the catchy phrase was hers and not his. Yet, since the 1920s, it's usually attributed to Voltaire.

> **"We traded a first-round draft choice for a twenty-eight-year-old flyswatter [Manute Bol] who could score only 1.9 points a game.... My grandmother could score two points a game, as long as she wasn't double-teamed."**
>
> *—Charles Barkley*

In one of the stranger accusations of misquoting, basketball great Barkley declared that his was misquoted...in his own autobiography. He allegedly tried to stop publication of the book and, when he couldn't, told an interviewer that his cowriter's job was to **"make the book controversial, to sell a lot of copies. Unfortunately, that's not fair to me."** The journalistic question remains: Is it okay to quote Barkley's bylined words, even if he later said they weren't his?

"**Unless we put Medical Freedom into the Constitution, the time will come when medicine will organize into an undercover dictatorship... The Constitution of this Republic should make special privilege for Medical Freedom as well as Religious Freedom.**"

—*Benjamin Rush*

The Declaration of Independence signer had a lot to say about medicine in early America. But he didn't say this, according to scholars. It seems that an 1801 lecture at the University of Pennsylvania was embellished and modified over the years, primarily by Dr. A. C. Cowperthwaite and others who merged the two doctors' ideas. The fact that the word "undercover" wasn't in common usage until well after Rush's death should have been a tip-off. Said Rush biographer Stephen Fried, **"The quote was manipulated for medical-political reasons and gets re-manipulated through each version of managed care."**

"What the American people need is not more health care. What we need is more Jesus care."

—Mike Pence

The vice president may be against universal health care. But he's not the source of this quote, which was birthed on a **Fox News parody page** before being circulated far and wide, including an unquestioning appearance in HuffPost.

"All tyranny needs to gain a foothold is for people of good conscience to remain silent."

—*Thomas Jefferson*

When it comes to trusting a source on a quote by Thomas Jefferson, I'll take the good folks at Monticello, Jefferson's historic home, over other sources that started attributing it to him in 2005. They say it hasn't been found anywhere in the writings of the third President of the United States. **Edmund Burke** is often given credit as well. But sources show that it may actually be rooted in an 1867 speech where **John Stuart Mill** said, **"Bad men need nothing more to compass their ends than that good men should look on and do nothing."**

"Owning guns is not a right. If it were a right, it would be in the Constitution."

—*Alexandria Ocasio-Cortez*

It didn't take long for the youngest woman ever to be elected to Congress to face the wrath of false quotes—including this one, which seems to have set out to prove her ignorant of the Second Amendment. Memes have also put these words in her mouth: **"I'm speaking with myself, number one, because I have a very good brain and I've said a lot of things."** Who actually said that? **Donald Trump**.

"It bothers me that the intelligence of animals is measured by how willing they are to obey the commands of a human. Same goes for students in schools, innit?"

—*Ricky Gervais*

Here's how easy it can be to create misinformation. A Montreal writer set out to mock what he saw as the banality of Ricky Gervais's comedy, and he made a meme out of text he found on Reddit paired with a photo of the actor. The resulting tweet was shared by none other than Wikileaks founder **Julian Assange**, and it has been misattributed to Gervais ever since.

"The best way to teach your kids about taxes is by eating 30 percent of their ice cream."

—*Bill Murray*

Somehow, the parody account on Twitter with Bill Murray's picture and name on it has attracted more than 511,000 Twitter followers (as of this writing). Many of them, including CBSnews.com, reposted this as fact in spite of its source carrying this ineffectual disclaimer: **"I AM NOT BILL MURRAY. This is a parody account. This account is not in any way affiliated with the actor Bill Murray."**

"You can't go back and change the beginning, but you can start where you are and change the ending."

—*C. S. Lewis*

And, apparently, you can go back and change the byline for a pithy quote. In this case, motivational speaker **Zig Ziglar** did say it, but claimed to be quoting **Carl Bard**. Yet it's also been traced to **James R. Sherman** in his book *Rejection*. Complicating matters further, according to Quote Investigator a reporter noted it on a sign in **a Philadelphia Eagles locker room** sans source. Now you can find it followed by Ziglar, Bard, Lewis, and others. Who actually started the chain of misquotations is unclear.

"When you reach the end of your rope, tie a knot and hang on."

—*Franklin Delano Roosevelt/Thomas Jefferson/
Eleanor Roosevelt*

Before Thomas Jefferson began being credited for this one online, Franklin Roosevelt was cited as its source. A *Chicken Soup for the Soul* book even attributed it to Eleanor Roosevelt. But the first documented source of its appearance was in an Oklahoma newspaper in 1920. Who said it? The writer, alas, was **anonymous**.

"I love my cigar, but I take it out of my mouth once in a while."

—*Groucho Marx*

Legend—and many books about the Groucho with and without his brothers—has it that Marx was interviewing a contestant on his game show. The contestant had a very large family and, when asked about it, commented **"Well, I love my husband."** The quote above was supposedly his response. Stories traveled that the exchange was censored from the broadcast and the story persisted. But there's no record of it and Marx denied that it ever happened. One possible explanation is that the story grew out of a G-rated version with a different guest—a woman with sixteen siblings. "Oh, my daddy loves children," she said, to which he is documented having responded. **"Well, I like pancakes, but I haven't got closetsful of them."**

"Sometimes a cigar is just a cigar" or "Gentlemen, there are times when a cigar is only a cigar!"

—*Sigmund Freud*

Close, but, well, no cigar. Most historians agree that these quotes are apocryphal and there is no real evidence that Freud ever uttered these words. Of course, he is known for writing about the phallic symbolism of smoking, and he was often photographed while smoking a cigar. A biographer noted that the good doctor was often so grumpy with men who did not smoke that his acolytes felt pressured to become cigar smokers. Attributions of this probable misquotation only crop up in the literature of the 1950s, more than a decade after Freud's death in 1939. Flimsily cited versions appeared in medical journals and a cigar smoking magazine, and, in the *American Historical Review*, Peter Gay wrote (without citation), **"After all, as Sigmund Freud once said, there are times when a man craves a cigar simply because he wants a good smoke!"** Freud may have been rather touchy about his own rather intense nicotine addiction, but there is no hard evidence that he actually said these famous words.

"I wish I'd done everything on Earth with you."

—*F. Scott Fitzgerald*

Here's a way to trap an English student trying to take a shortcut. While the quote above is often attributed to Fitzgerald, and sometimes includes his novel *The Great Gatsby* as its source, sorry, freshman who put it on a term paper: The quote doesn't come from F. Scott Fitzgerald or his novel. It comes from the **Baz Luhrmann** film version

"For sale. Baby shoes. Never worn."

—Ernest Hemingway

The story—and it's a good one—is that Hemingway accepted a bet that he could write a six-word short story. The result was the six words above. And while the anecdote has been shared in many a writing class as well as in a play about the famed author, there's no evidence that the competition ever happened or that those were Hemingway's words.

"If I were to run, I'd run as a Republican. They're the dumbest group of voters in the country. They believe anything on Fox News. I could lie and they'd still eat it up. I bet my numbers would be terrific."

—*Donald Trump*

While he said a lot of quotable things before, during, and after his run for president, this isn't one of them. He didn't say it in *People* magazine, the source often linked to the quote, or anywhere else. In this case, journalists spent a significant amount of time discrediting the viral meme rather than stating it as fact.

"A billion here, a billion there, pretty soon, you're talking real money."

—*Everett Dirksen*

Although it claimed a third of inquiries had to do with this quote, The Dirksen Congressional Center insists that there's no evidence that he actually said it. After digging through clippings, audio tapes, and more than 12,000 pages of his notes, its researchers concluded **"the late Senate Minority Leader certainly would have endorsed the meaning behind the phrase, but it is questionable that he ever coined it"** — in spite of what you may have read (sometimes with "million" instead "billion") in *The Lexington Herald Leader* and other papers.

"I cannot be part of a world where men dress their wives as prostitutes by showing everything that should be cherished...."

—*Keanu Reeves*

It's tough to figuring out the thinking behind this one. Someone, somewhere, took a lengthy quote bemoaning not just the way women dress, but also men spending money in nightclubs, people who don't understand religion, and those who trick out their cars—and decided to attribute it to Ted of *Bill and Ted's Excellent Adventure*. As Ted would say, the quote is **totally bogus**.

"Not tonight, Josephine."

—*Napoleon Bonaparte*

Okay, so it's a simple enough phrase that he might have said it. But there's no documentation. But it became part of popular lore after actress Florrie Forde sang a tune by that title penned by **Worton David** and **Lawrence Wright**.

"**America is morally upside down because the wealthiest 1 percent tricked the dumbest 20 percent into believing the rest of us are so evil that lying to us and cheating us is not only okay, it's godly.**"

—*Jim Carrey*

The rubber-faced actor has made no secret about his contempt from **Donald Trump**. But there's no evidence to indicate that Carrey said or wrote these words about the powers that be—despite the proliferation of memes putting quotation marks around it and pairing it with his photo.

"You do not have a soul. You are a soul. You have a body."

—C. S. Lewis

The quote—which has never been found in the author's collected works and letters—predates him by a few decades or more. The website Mere Orthodoxy found a version of it not only in the 1959 novel *A Canticle for Leibowitz* but also in a 1905 periodical, a 1901 YMCA manual, and in British documents from the 1800s.

"In the end, it is not the years in your life that count, it's the life in your years."

—Abraham Lincoln

Quote Investigator writes this one off as something that could well have been penned by an advertising copywriter. It certainly wasn't Lincoln. Still, that didn't stop the GOP from crediting it to him in a 2017 tweet. **No reference to the quote—by anyone—predates 1947.**

"Give me six hours to cut down a tree and I will spend the first four sharpening the axe."

—*Abraham Lincoln*

First, let's consider the logic: A champion tree feller can down a twelve-inch pine in about that many seconds. Lincoln would surely have known that that six hours is a mighty long stretch of time for the task. **Which is why it should come as no surprise that there's no documentation of Abe having actually said this.** The ideas are present in an 1856 sermon, but a version of the quote wasn't credited to the president until 1960. All that being said, it is a good idea to sharpen your axe first.

"Make the trains run on time."

—*Benito Mussolini*

While it's the expression most commonly affixed to the Italian dictator, *The Oxford Dictionary of Quotations* says he never quite put it that way—although he was quoted as saying, **"We must leave exactly on time.... From now on everything must function to perfection."**

"Insanity is doing the same thing over and over again and expecting different results."

—*Albert Einstein*

While that Princeton genius didn't actually say it, sometimes it seems like everyone in Washington has. The quote is used over and over again by politicians and journalists to criticize what they see as repeated mistakes—usually committed by others, of course.

"You are braver than you believe, you are stronger than you seem, and you are smarter than you think."

—A. A. Milne

While *Newsday* credited this inspirational line to the creator of Winnie-the-Pooh, this and many other Hundred Acre Woods quotes go to the writers of Pooh scripts that were filmed long after Milne's death. In this case, it's from 1997's *Pooh's Grand Adventure: The Search for Christopher Robin*. (Before you tattoo any Pooh quote on your arm—which is actually a thing some people do—you might want to verify it via the Pooh Misquoted website.)

"The harder I work, the luckier I get."

—Thomas Jefferson

And no matter how hard you look, you won't find any real source indicating that the third President of the United States actually said this. Versions have also been attributed to movie mogul **Samuel Goldwyn**, golfer **Gary Player**, basketball coach **Dick Motta**, and inventor **Charles Kettering**.

"If I've lost Cronkite, I've lost Middle America."

—Lyndon Johnson

It's still being quoted—even in newspapers as big as *The Toronto Star*—as evidence of a president's realization of the impact of the media on popular opinion. But there's no evidence that LBJ made the statement, let alone put that much stock in what the then-most-popular TV news anchor said about the war in Vietnam. (For the record, Cronkite called it **"a stalemate."**) And if he did say something like the now-famous quote, Johnson didn't act on it. In the weeks after Cronkite's on-air comment, Johnson continued to defend—and increase—United States military involvement in Vietnam.

"I mourn the loss of thousands of precious lives, but I will not rejoice in the death of one, not even an enemy."

—*Martin Luther King Jr.*

While Dr. King did say that **"Returning hate for hate multiplies hate,"** he isn't responsible for this quote, which has often prefaced it. Those words actually came from a Facebook user, **Jessica Dovey**, who accurately used quotation marks to separate King's quote from hers—quotation marks that seem to have disappeared in later postings.

"Nonstop pursuit of wealth will only turn a person into a twisted being, just like me."

—*Steve Jobs*

Those would be some intense deathbed words—if they were actually said. These and a long list of other would-be Jobsian observations, didn't start circulating until years after his death. And they bear no relation to the final words observed and reported by his sister: **"Oh wow, oh wow, oh wow."**

"Be the change you wish to see in the world."

—Mahatma Gandhi

It's no wonder this quote has long been attached to gazillions of T-shirts, wall decals, and Lucite desk clutter. Problem is, there's no record of Gandhi ever actually saying it. What he did say would be far more difficult to fit on a coffee mug: **"If we could change ourselves, the tendencies in the world would also change. As a man changes his own nature, so does the attitude of the world change towards him."**

"The only thing necessary for the triumph of evil is for good men to do nothing."

—*Edmund Burke*

There are many variations on this quote floating out there—perhaps due to the fact that there's no evidence that Burke ever actually said or wrote it. When you don't have an original, the variations can vary wildly. And when even President Kennedy gives the wrong source, it's easy to believe its accuracy. What did Burke actually have to say about evil and good? Well, there's this: **"When bad men combine, the good must associate; else they will fall one by one, an unpitied sacrifice in a contemptible struggle."**

"If the NBA isn't rigging the finals, they should at least investigate these refs for taking bribes or gambling...trust me, I've been investigated for less."

—*Tom Brady*

Why should the New England Patriots' star quarterback call attention to his own questionable actions and go after basketball referees? The point is moot because he didn't. **This meme was generated by sports satire Instagram @Grrindtime.**

"Always remember that you are absolutely unique. Just like everyone else."

—*Margaret Mead*

It was labeled **"Meade's Maxim"** in the book *1,001 Logical Laws, Accurate Axioms, Profound Principles, Trusty Truisms, Homey Homilies, Colorful Corollaries, Quotable Quotes, and Rambunctious Ruminations for All Walks of Life*. But note the misspelling of her name. There's no indication that the anthropologist actually said this.

"There are no strangers here; only friends you haven't yet met."

—*William Butler Yeats*

You can tell when a publication opts not to do its homework when it used the phrase "widely attributed to." In this case, the phrase "widely attributed to William Butler Yeats" in a Guinness-sponsored section of *The New York Times* is the chummy quote above. Yet nobody has yet come up with a direct link to Yeats. More likely it evolved from a poem by **Edgar Guest**, who wrote, **"That strangers are friends that we some day may meet."**

Carl Sagan J. K. Rowling Confucius Jay
Audrey Hepburn C. S. Lewis Betty Wh
Ricky Gervais Charles Manson Bill Gates
Seuss P. T. Barnum Bill Murray Drake To
Brady Marilyn Monroe Barack Obama W.
B. Du Bois Mahatma Gandhi Keanu Reev
Alexandria Ocasio-Cortez Aristotle Jos
Stalin Donald Trump Dr. Martin Luth
King, Jr. Benjamin Franklin Outkast Glo
Steinem Banksy A. A. Milne Kurt Vonneg
Jr. George Carlin Susan B. Anthony Ben
Mussolini Meryl Streep The Bible Muhamm
Ali Taylor Swift Henry David Thore
George Washington Darth Vader Abraha
Lincoln William Tecumseh Sherman Fra
Zappa Mr. Spock (Leonard Nimoy) Elean
Roosevelt Gordon Gecko (Michael Dougla
Oprah Winfrey William Shakespeare K
Cobain Sun Tzu Maya Angelou Buddha E
Peron Isaac Newton Ann Richards Lau
Anderson Mike Pence Tarzan Ralph Wal
Emerson Steve Martin Ambrose Bier
Captain Kirk (William Shatner) Anne Pl
Franz Kafka Nelson Mandela Bob Dyl
Thomas Jefferson Kanye West Volta
Niccolò Machiavelli Rick Blaine (Humphr
Bogart) Barack Obama Thomas Edis
The Bhagavad Gita Harriet Tubman
Scott Fitzgerald Steve Jobs Jack Ker

THEY DIDN'T SAY IT FIRST

Quoting a quoter isn't the same as quoting a source. It's quotation once removed. But that hasn't stopped credit from being doled out to quote quoters galore.

"A woman needs a man like a fish needs a bicycle."

—*Gloria Steinem*

Steinem did say it. She just didn't originate it. In fact, she wrote a letter to *Time* magazine in 2000 correcting it. "In fact," she wrote, "**Irina Dunn**, a distinguished Australian educator, journalist and politician, coined the phrase back in 1970 when she was a student at the University of Sydney. She paraphrased the philosopher who said, 'Man needs God like fish needs a bicycle.' Dunn deserves credit for creating such a popular and durable spoof of the old idea that women need men more than vice versa."

"Hell has no fury like a woman scorned."

—William Congreve

Sure, the playwright did say that. Or, at least, he wrote something close to it. (**"Nor hell a fury, like a woman scorn'd."**) But the idea goes back a bit further, to **Colley Cibber** who, a year earlier, had a stage character say, **"No fiend in hell can match the fury of a disappointed woman."**

"Art should comfort the disturbed and disturb the comfortable."

—*Banksy*

GQ and other publications may celebrate these words as coming from the mind of the norm-challenging artist, but the notion didn't spring fresh from Banksy's brain. It's actually a variation on the words of **Finley Peter Dunne**'s bartender character Mr. Dooley. In a 1902 book, Dunne/Dooley wrote: **"Th' newspaper does ivrything f'r us. It runs th' polis foorce an' th' banks, commands th' milishy, controls th' ligislachure, baptizes th' young, marries th' foolish, comforts th' afflicted, afflicts th' comfortable, buries th' dead an' roasts thim aftherward."**

"A ship in harbor is safe, but that is not what ships are built for."

—*Grace M. Hopper*

She may have popularized the expression, but the inspirational Navy Rear Admiral was actually quoting **John A. Shedd**, who included it in his book *Salt from My Attic*. Whether he conceived it himself or was quoting wisdom passed down to him is unknown.

"Military intelligence is a contradiction in terms."

—*Groucho Marx* or *George Carlin*

When you think about the great wits of the twentieth century, the moustached Marx brother and the class clown George Carlin certainly make the short list. But they aren't the ones who first spouted this aphorism. That man was Brigadier-General **John Charteris**, a British intelligence officer during World War I.

"A riddle wrapped in an mystery inside an enigma."

—*Richard Burton*

Actor Richard Burton earned attention for saying something similar: "a secret wrapped in an enigma inside a mystery" about his on again/off again wife Elizabeth Taylor. But the source of the Russian stacking doll-ish quote is actually **Winston Churchill**, who colorfully used it to describe...Russia.

"Winning isn't everything. It's the only thing."

—*Vince Lombardi*

He's been quoted as saying this. And "Winning isn't everything but wanting to win is." And "Winning isn't everything, but the will to win is everything." And while Lombardi has one or more of these variations, he wasn't the first to this adage. That seems to have been UCLA coach **Henry Russell "Red" Sanders**.

"Some men see things as they are and say, why; I dream things that never were and say, why not."

—Robert Kennedy

Inspiring words? Yes, indeed. But they derive from lines said in a very different context. In George Bernard Shaw's play *Back to Methuselah*, the serpent says to Eve in the Garden of Eden, **"You see things; and you say 'Why?' But I dream things that never were; and I say 'Why not?'"**

"Resistance to tyranny is obedience to God."

—*Susan B. Anthony*

The women's rights leader did use the phrase but credited it as an old revolutionary maxim. **Benjamin Franklin** also occasionally gets a shout-out for saying it. But it actually predates the United States, going back as far as 1688 and Massachusetts governor **Simon Bradstreet**.

"A woman is like a tea bag— you never know how strong she is until she gets in hot water."

—*Nancy Reagan*

Although it's been attributed to many people in addition to the former first lady. In fact, it's been attributed to even more former first lady **Eleanor Roosevelt**. But there's no indication that either woman initiated the phrase. Nor did conservative activist **Phyllis Schlafly** or columnist **Earl Wilson**.

"Age is an issue of mind over matter. If you don't mind, it doesn't matter."

—Muhammad Ali

There are plenty of things that Ali said that are memorable. And he did, in fact, use this line with a reporter for *The San Diego Union*. But he certainly didn't originate it since it was already credited to comedian **Jack Benny** and baseball great **Satchel Paige**. Who actually said it first? That remains a mystery. And, perhaps, it doesn't matter.

"Failing to prepare is preparing to fail."

—*John Wooden*

The first person to make it into the Basketball Hall of Fame as both a player and a coach has a long list of inspirational quotes to his credit (including **"Failure is not fatal but failure to change might be"**). But, in this case, he was only quoting an older saying—which didn't prevent the UCLA newsroom from giving him credit.

"The death of one man is a tragedy. The death of millions is a statistic."

—Josef Stalin

It certainly fits the contemporary image of the Russian leader. But, even if he did say it (that's in dispute), he didn't say it first. A likely source is German satirist **Kurt Tucholsky** who put the words in the mouth of a fictional diplomat.

"The best government is that which governs least."

—Henry David Thoreau

Thoreau did paraphrase the line in his *Resistance to Civil Government* (aka *Civil Disobedience*). But he was paraphrasing the motto of publisher John L. O'Sullivan's *The United States Magazine and Democratic Review*. Thoreau's version: **"That government is best that governs least."** Side note: the quote has also been credited to **Thomas Jefferson**, who did not say it but may have felt it.

Carl Sagan J. K. Rowling Confucius Jay
Audrey Hepburn C. S. Lewis Betty Wh
Ricky Gervais Charles Manson Bill Gates
Seuss P. T. Barnum Bill Murray Drake To
Brady Marilyn Monroe Barack Obama W
B. Du Bois Mahatma Gandhi Keanu Reev
Alexandria Ocasio-Cortez Aristotle Jo
Stalin Donald Trump Dr. Martin Luth
King, Jr. Benjamin Franklin Outkast Glo
Steinem Banksy A. A. Milne Kurt Vonneg
Jr. George Carlin Susan B. Anthony Ben
Mussolini Meryl Streep The Bible Muhamm
Ali Taylor Swift Henry David Thore
George Washington Darth Vader Abrah
Lincoln William Tecumseh Sherman Fra
Zappa Mr. Spock (Leonard Nimoy) Elea
Roosevelt Gordon Gecko (Michael Dougl
Oprah Winfrey William Shakespeare K
Cobain Sun Tzu Maya Angelou Buddha E
Peron Isaac Newton Ann Richards Lau
Anderson Mike Pence Tarzan Ralph Wal
Emerson Steve Martin Ambrose Bier
Captain Kirk (William Shatner) Anne R
Franz Kafka Nelson Mandela Bob Dyl
Thomas Jefferson Kanye West Volta
Niccolo Machiavelli Rick Blaine (Humphr
Bogart) Barack Obama Thomas Edis
The Bhagavad Gita Harriet Tubman
Scott Fitzgerald Steve Jobs Jack Ke

THAT'S NOT WHAT THEY SAID

So close. Sometimes a quote *almost* gets it right. But a missing word or clarifying phrase can make a big difference. On the other hand, being the person who corrects such minor discrepancies can make you really annoying to watch movies with.

"War is hell."

—*William Tecumseh Sherman*

The Civil War general captured this feeling but did it in a few more words than are usually quoted. What he actually said to an audience in Ohio was, **"There is many a boy here today who looks on war as all glory, but, boys, it is all hell. You can bear this warning voice to generations yet to come."**

"Spare the rod, spoil the child."

—*The Bible*

The "spare the rod" part is in there. But the "spoil the child" is not—at least not in quotations that haven't been modernized. Most offer some variation on **"He that spareth his rod hateth his son: but he that loveth him chasteneth him betimes."**

"A dingo ate my baby."

—Lindy Chamberlain

Jokes on *The Simpsons*, *Seinfeld*, and more transformed the *A Cry in the Dark* movie line to the quote above. What Chamberlain (played by Meryl Streep) actually said in the film, though, was, **"The dingo's got my baby."**

"Luke, I am your father."

—Darth Vader

Visit your nearest science fiction convention and try uttering that line allegedly from *The Empire Strikes Back*. No doubt you will have a lineup of Anakin wannabes correcting you. What Vader (voiced by James Earl Jones) actually says in the film (screenplay by Lawrence Kasdan and Leigh Brackett from a story by George Lucas) is **"No, I am your father."**

"You can paint a pretty picture, but you can't predict the weather."

—*Outkast*

Singing "paint a pretty picture" might sound amazing when you belt it out at karaoke, but the correct words written by Andre 3000 make a lot more actual sense. If you listen closely, you can hear him say **"you can plan a pretty picnic."** Please, give Miss Jackson our deepest apologies.

"Spanish girls love me like I'm on Twitter."

—Drake

Sometimes a lesser-known reference will be replaced in listeners' minds with a more familiar one—even if the change doesn't make sense. In "The Motto," Drake actually rapped **"Spanish girls love me like I'm Aventura"**—which is a Miami suburb, a mall, and a Bacheta band. Take your pick.

"Beam me up, Scotty!"

—*Captain Kirk*

As any dedicated Trekkie will tell you, William Shatner's Captain Kirk never really said this phrase on the original *Star Trek*. What he did in fact say was, **"Scotty, beam us up, fast!"** and, on one occasion, **"Scotty, beam me up."** Perhaps it was Shatner's signature staccato delivery that confused everyone's ears in the first place.

"It's life, Jim, but not as we know it."

—*Mr. Spock*

And while we're on the subject of *Star Trek*, Mr. Spock (played by Leonard Nimoy) never said this oft-repeated (elsewhere) phrase. Its use in the novelty song **"Star Trekkin'"** by The Firm help cement it into geek culture.

"Greed is good."

—Gordon Gecko

Yes, those three words sum up the philosophy of the high-end trader (played by Michael Douglas) in Oliver Stone's attention-grabbing film ***Wall Street***. But he never quite said it that succinctly. What Gecko actually concludes, in a lengthy speech to stockholders, is **"The point is, ladies and gentleman, that greed—for lack of a better word—is good. Greed is right. Greed works."**

"Good things come to those who wait."

—*Violet Fane*

Often used interchangeably with "all things come to those who wait," this phrase isn't quite complete. Consider the full verse of the Violet Fane (aka Lady Mary Montgomerie Currie) poem it comes from: **"'Ah, all things come to those who wait,' / (I say these words to make me glad), / But something answers soft and sad, / 'They come, but often come too late.'"** Which suggests that waiting around may not always be the best option.

"Blood is thicker than water."

—The Bible

Often used to support the idea that family bonds are more important and stronger than the connections between friends and acquaintances, this is one of the more commonly altered quotes in the Good Book. What it actually says is, **"The blood of the covenant is thicker than the water of the womb,"** which doesn't mean that at all. Rather, it makes a case for connection between comrades being stronger than kin. So this one has flip-flopped through the ages.

"The seven deadly sins."

—The Bible

Yes, the book lists gluttony, greed, sloth, lust, vanity, envy, and wrath, saying that the Lord hates them and that they are an **"abomination to him."** But nowhere in Proverbs or elsewhere does it say that they are deadly.

"If you build it, they will come."

—The Voice in Field of Dreams

Spoiler alert: Yes, he builds it. And, yes, a number of no-longer-living baseball players show up. But the mysterious voice in the sports movie that rivals *Brian's Song* for making tough guys cry doesn't actually say it quite that way. Actually, he states that **"If you build it, he will come."**

"That's one small step for man, one giant leap for mankind."

—*Neil Armstrong*

It may seem like nitpicking. But given the magnitude of the event—a human being setting foot on the moon for the first time—and the frequency of the line being quoted, you'd think that there would be no dispute about what was actually said when Neil Armstrong took his famous step. Yet the astronaut himself insisted, contrary to what people believe they heard back on the home planet, that he actually said, **"That's one small step for a man..."** And, when you think about it, the quote makes a lot more sense with the article "a" included.

"Money is the root of all evil."

—*The Bible*

A few words are often dropped from this oft-used biblical phrase. The line from 1 Timothy is, depending on your translation, more along the lines of **"For the love of money is the root of all evil"** or "root for all kinds of evil is the love of money." It's the greed, not the money itself, that is being frowned on—which gives the wealthy a bit of salvation leeway.

"The devil is in the details."

—Ludwig Mies Van Der Rohe

What the architect actually said was: **"God is in the details."** And, even then, he wasn't being terribly original. Some take it back further, though *Bartlett's Familiar Quotations* lists it as anonymous. Others attribute it to an old German proverb ("Der liebe Gott steckt im detail").

"I am not a crook. I have never been a crook. I don't even even know what a crook looks like."

—*Richard Nixon*

Well, about a third of it is close to the truth. What Nixon actually said was, **"People have got to know whether or not their president is a crook. Well, I'm not a crook. I've earned everything I've got."**

"Lucy, you've got some 'splaining to do!"

—Ricky Ricardo

In 180 episodes over six seasons of *I Love Lucy*, no matter how frustrated he got with his wife, Lucy, Ricky Ricardo (played by Desi Arnaz) never exactly said the quote most often associated with him. But try telling that to the meme makers, let alone the writers who have put it on the list of top TV catchphrases. (Granted, he did offer such almosts as, **"OK, 'splain."**)

"Water, water everywhere/ and not a drop to drink."

—*Samuel Taylor Coleridge*

The actual lines in Coleridge's famous poem "The Rime of the Ancient Mariner" are a bit different: **"Water, water, everywhere / Nor any drop to drink."**

"Water is not a human right."

—*Peter Brabeck-Letmathe*

Pretty harsh if the Nestlé chairman/CEO actually said it, right? He didn't, but what he actually did say, according to Snopes, isn't as brief nor is it significantly different: **"The one opinion, which I think is extreme, is represented by the NGOs, who bang on about declaring water a public right. That means that as a human being you should have a right to water. That's an extreme solution. The other view says that water is a foodstuff like any other, and like any other foodstuff it should have a market value. Personally, I believe it's better to give a foodstuff a value so that we're all aware it has its price, and then that one should take specific measures for the part of the population that has no access to this water, and there are many different possibilities there."**

"Mrs. Robinson, are you trying to seduce me?"

—*Benjamin Braddock*

The answer, of course, is yes. But that's not exactly what Dustin Hoffman's character says in the classic 1967 film *The Graduate*. The hapless Braddock, framed by Mrs. Robinson's leg, actually asks **"Mrs. Robinson, you're trying to seduce me, aren't you?"**

"Walk softly and carry a big stick."

— *Theodore Roosevelt*

The first-time then-governor of New York Theodore Roosevelt articulated his soon-to-be-famous diplomatic philosophy, he gave due credit. **"I have always been fond of the West African proverb: 'Speak softly and carry a big stick; you will go far,'"** he was quoted as saying in 1900. Later, he referred to it as an "old proverb." While the quote is often misstated as "Walk softly," there's also a possibility that Roosevelt himself is misattributing it. No record has been found of the quote—in West Africa or elsewhere—being used before he used it.

"Badges? We don't need no stinking badges."

—*Gold Hat*

Here's the road this one took into the pop culture vernacular. In the novel *The Treasure of the Sierra Madre* by B. Traven, the line is written: **"Badges, to god-damned hell with badges! We have no badges. In fact, we don't need badges. I don't have to show you any stinking badges, you god-damned cabron and chinga tu madre."** The classic 1948 film toned it down a bit. Gold Hat (played by Alfonso Bedoya) says, "Badges? We ain't got no badges. We don't need·no badges. I don't have to show you any stinkin' badges!" But you can blame **Mel Brooks** for the current version. In his film *Blazing Saddles*, he reduced it to the now-commonly quoted "Badges? We don't need no stinking badges."

"Just the facts, ma'am."

—*Joe Friday*

Dragnet, the ultra-serious police procedural show that promised that "The story you are about to see is true..." was a TV staple in the 1950s and, later, in reruns, spin-offs, and spoofs. Sargent Friday (played by Jack Webb) did, in fact, utter such phrases as "**All we want are the facts, ma'am,**" and **"All we know are the facts, ma'am,"** but this specific turn of phrase, according to Snopes, was transformed thanks to humorist **Stan Freberg** and scores of journalists writing about the show.

"Genius is 1 percent inspiration and 99 percent perspiration."

—Thomas Edison

The Wizard of Menlo Park did, in fact, say something like this. At first, the quote had a 2 percent to 98 percent ratio but was later upgraded/downgraded to 1 percent to 99 percent in a later biography. But the root of the idea belongs to essayist **Kate Sanborn**, who predated Edison with **"Genius is inspiration, talent is perspiration."** Later, she wrote of Edison's quote, "I had never heard that definition and thought it was mine. Of late it has been widely quoted, but with no acknowledgment, so I still think it is mine."

"I invented the internet."

—*Al Gore*

When it comes to politics, it's no surprise when a candidate is attacked for something allegedly said and then exaggerated. And so, amplified by late-night comics, Vice President—and wannabe POTUS—Gore became known for taking sole credit for a technological/communication revolution. Clearly, that's absurd. But he did say that **"during my service in the United States Congress, I took the initiative in creating the internet."** (Snopes compares it to President Eisenhower taking the initiative in creating the interstate highway system—which doesn't mean he invented highways.) Gore-sponsored legislation did lead to the linking of universities and libraries as well as the ability to commercially use the system.

"Houston, we have a problem."

—John Swigert

In space, apparently, no one can quote you accurately. The famous understatement is actually a variation on what was said by two Apollo 13 crew members. First, astronaut John Swigert said, **"OK, Houston, we've had a problem here,"** and, when asked to repeat, fellow astronaut Jim Lovell chimed in: **"Uh, Houston, we've had a problem."**

"On the whole, I would rather be in Philadelphia."

—*W. C. Fields*

There are many out there who believe that this quote is inscribed on the tombstone of the legendary screen comic. But his grave marker is actually quite simple. The story seems to have arisen from a 1925 article in *Vanity Fair* magazine in which famous folks were asked to write their own epitaphs. Offered Fields—or, possibly, a publicist—**"Here Lies W. C. Fields: I would rather be living in Philadelphia."**

"[I]...did everything he did... backwards and in high heels."

—*Ginger Rogers*

Her dance partnership with Fred Astaire led to cinematic magic. And, yes, her skills were often not as appreciated as those of his. But the line attributed to her was actually the words of cartoonist **Bob Thaves**, who offered this appreciation in his *Frank and Ernest* series. Side note: Rogers herself, in her autobiography, said she usually practiced in low heels.

"Why don't you come up and see me sometime?"

—*Lady Lou*

The ahead-of-her-time characters played by **Mae West** made some provocative statements. And this is *almost* one of them. What she actually said in the 1933 film *She Done Him Wrong* is **"Why don't you come up sometime and see me?"**

"Mirror, Mirror on the wall."

—*The Queen in* Snow White and the Seven Dwarfs

So, so close. What the dark-hearted one actually said was: "Magic mirror on the wall." And then, when she believed she had taken care of her rival, she asked, **"Magic Mirror on the wall, who now is the fairest one of all?"**

"Bubble, bubble, toil and trouble."

—The Weird Sisters

No, that's **"double, double, toil and trouble."**
And, side note, in the First Folio editions of William Shakespeare's *Macbeth* the three witches are called "wayward" not "weird" sisters.

"A little knowledge is a dangerous thing."

—Alexander Pope

Actually, what Pope said was: **"A little learning is a dangerous thing,"** further adding, poetically, "drink deep, or taste not the Pierian spring: there shallow draughts intoxicate the brain, and drinking largely sobers us again." The substitution of "learning" for "knowledge" came from a misquote in a 1774 magazine. Some take it back even further, to Sir Francis Bacon, who said **"A little philosophy inclineth man's mind to atheism; but depth in philosophy bringeth men's minds about to religion"**—a quote later altered by an anonymous letter writer to say "'Twas well observed by my Lord Bacon, that a little knowledge is apt to puff up, and make men giddy, but a greater share of it will set them right, and bring them to low and humble thoughts of themselves."

"You want the truth? You can't handle the truth."

—Colonel Jessup

It's become one of the most famous cinematic lines from the 1990s, even if few people remember the plot details of the film it came from. But Jack Nicholson's courtroom outburst in the Aaron Sorkin–penned **A Few Good Men** isn't nearly as one-sided as it's usually memed.

In the film, it's actually a dialogue scene that goes like this:

Nicholson: "You want answers?"

Cruise: "I want the truth."

Nicholson: "You can't handle the truth."

The question is: Now that you know the truth about the quote, can you handle getting it right next time you try out your Nicholson impression?

"Somebody tells you they love you, you got to believe 'em."

—*Taylor Swift*

Here's a misquoter who should have known better. The incorrect lyric, above, was used in an SAT practice test published by The Princeton Review as an example of incorrect grammar. The only problem: Swift's actual lyric, **"Somebody tells you they love you, you're gonna believe them"** is actually grammatically correct. Swift's Tumblr response: "Not the right lyrics at all pssshhhh. You had one job, test people. One job."

"If you have to ask how much it costs, you can't afford one."

—*J. P. Morgan*

According to The Quote Verifier website, Morgan not only didn't say this, he probably couldn't put together words so succinctly. Morgan biographer Jean Strouse does, however, give credence to an anecdote that has Morgan responding to Henry Clay Pierce's query about luxury boating prices with **"You have no right to own a yacht if you ask that question."**

"I love the smell of napalm in the morning. It smells like... victory."

—*Bill Kilgore*

It's a bold, dramatic moment in Francis Ford Coppola's epic Vietnam film *Apocalypse Now*—only it's actually more than just a moment, with more dialogue between "morning" and "It." What the shirtless Kilgore (played by Robert Duvall) actually says is: **"You smell that? Do you smell that? Napalm, son. Nothing else in the world smells like that. I love the smell of napalm in the morning. You know, one time we had a hill bombed, for twelve hours. When it was all over, I walked up. We didn't find one of 'em, not one stinkin' dink body. The smell, you know that gasoline smell, the whole hill. Smelled like...victory."**

"My country, right or wrong."

—*Carl Schurz*

German immigrant and Civil War brigadier general, and United States senator Carl Schurz is best known today for that divisive quote, which reads as patriotic or narrow-minded, depending on your politics. His actual quote, though, carried a little more nuance and was more proactive. What he said was: **"My country, right or wrong; if right, to be kept right; and if wrong, to be set right."** Essayist G. K. Chesterton did, in fact, retort in his book *The Defendant*: "'My country, right or wrong' is a thing no patriot would think of saying. It is like saying 'My mother, drunk or sober.'"

"Reports of my death have been greatly exaggerated."

—*Mark Twain*

And so have the words that Twain actually said. Yes, a journalist inquired about his health. His response: **"I can understand perfectly how the report of my illness got about, I have even heard on good authority that I was dead. James Ross Clemens, a cousin of mine, was seriously ill two or three weeks ago in London but is well now. The report of my illness grew out of his illness. The report of my death was an exaggeration."** The apocryphal version began appearing in print after his death.

"Facts are stupid things."

—Ronald Reagan

Well, at least Reagan didn't mean to say it. And he quickly corrected himself. What the president was trying to do was to quote John Adams, who said, "Facts are stubborn things; and whatever may be our wishes, our inclinations, or the dictates of our passions, they cannot alter the states of facts and evidence." What Reagan did say, in a speech to the 1988 Republican National Convention was, **"Facts are stupid things—stubborn things, should I say."** This didn't keep his slip from going down in pop-culture history and appearing in countless memes, as well as in *Parade* and *Salon*..

"Do you feel lucky, punk?"

—*Harry Callahan*

When you are looking down the barrel of Clint Eastwood's gun, it would be understandable if you didn't get his words down exactly right. But it wasn't just the "punk" who heard them in the 1971 thriller *Dirty Harry*, it was millions of moviegoers. What Dirty Harry actually said was, **"You've got to ask yourself one question. Do I feel lucky? Well, do ya, punk?"**

"Hello, Clarice."

—Hannibal Lecter

It's the go-to line when it comes time to make cannibal jokes. But cinema purists will throw it right back at you, noting that what the bad doctor (played by Anthony Hopkins) actually said in *Silence of the Lambs* was just **"Good evening, Clarice."** A small difference, perhaps, but the real line doesn't come across quite as terrifying.

"Children wish fathers looked but with their eyes; fathers that children with their judgment looked; and either may be wrong."

—*William Shakespeare*

Accept no substitutions. While Shakespeare *kinda* said this in *A Midsummer Night's Dream* (**"I would my father looked but with my eyes. I wish my father could see them with my eyes. Rather your eyes must with his judgment look."**), the quote as stated—and reposted—comes from *Aphorisms from Shakespeare*, a book from the late 1800s that edited, tweaked, and otherwise messed up the originals.

"I'm not the man I thought I was and I better be that man for my children."

—Jay-Z

Well, not exactly. What Jay-Z really said in his song "4:44" was the similarly themed, **"And if my children knew / I don't even know what I would do / If they ain't look at me the same / I would probably die with all the shame."** Why the mix-up? Blame that—and a lot of other things—on Harvey Weinstein, whose statement on his sexual harassment allegations included what he *said* were the words of Jay-Z.

"Lead on, Macduff."

—*Macbeth*

In fact it is **"Lay on, Macduff,"** in William Shakespeare's *Macbeth*, with the misquoted version boosted by its appearance in H. Rider Haggard's popular novel *King Solomon's Mines*.

"Alas, poor Yorick! I knew him well."

—*Hamlet*

What might be Hamlet's second most famous soliloquy actually begins: **"Alas, poor Yorick! I knew him, Horatio; a fellow of infinite jest, of most excellent fancy; he hath borne me on his back a thousand times; and now, how abhorred in my imagination it is!"** (William Shakespeare, *Hamlet*, Act 5, Scene 1). You could summarize all that as knowing him "well," but then you'd be taking all the joy out of the original Shakespeare.

"The only good Indian is a dead Indian."

—*Philip Sheridan*

In this case, the quote is just as bad as the misquote. What he is reported to have actually said is **"The only good Indians I ever saw were dead."** The general, however, denied having said that. Whether or not Sheridan said it, the follow-up from a higher-up is well documented. President Theodore Roosevelt, responding to the line, said, "I don't go so far as to think that the only good Indians are dead Indians, but I believe nine out of ten are, and I shouldn't like to inquire too closely into the case of the tenth."

"Racism will end when all the old white people die."

—Oprah Winfrey

That may be the case, but Winfrey didn't exactly say that. What she did say, to a BBC interviewer, was, **"As long as people can be judged by the color of their skin, the problem's not solved. As long as there are people who still... And there's a whole generation—I said this for apartheid South Africa, I said this for my own community in the South—there are still generations of people, older people, who were born and bred and marinated in it, in that prejudice and racism, and they just have to die."**

"We will all laugh at gilded butterflies."

—*King Lear*

If you are going to misquote Shakespeare, don't do it on a tattoo—as did actress/model Megan Fox. The actual lines are: **"We two alone will sing like birds i' the cage. When thou dost ask me blessing, I'll kneel down and ask of thee forgiveness: so we'll live, and pray, and sing, and tell old tales, and laugh at gilded butterflies, and hear poor rogues talk of court news; and we'll talk with them too."**

"You like me, you really like me!"

—Sally Field

How excited was Field when she won her second Oscar for Best Actress? Very. How often is her acceptance speech slightly misquoted? Very often. What she actually said was, **"I haven't had an orthodox career, and I've wanted more than anything to have your respect. The first time I didn't feel it, but this time I feel it, and I can't deny the fact that you like me, right now, you like me!"**

"Elementary, my dear Watson."

—*Sherlock Holmes*

Dig deep into the original Sir Arthur Conan Doyle short stories and novels, and you won't find this famous quote anywhere. Granted, in the story *The Adventure of the Crooked Man* you will find the words "my dear Watson" and "Elementary"— but there are no fewer than fifty-two words between them. And whereas **"My dear Watson"** is a common utterance throughout the series, **"elementary"** barely passes Holmes's lips. Where did the phrase come from then? Scholars think it was lifted from a P. G. Wodehouse story and popularized in the 1929 movie *The Return of Sherlock Holmes*.

"Play it again, Sam."

—Rick Blaine

So prevalent is this movie misquote that Woody Allen even made it the name of a play and, later, a movie. But although "Play it again, Sam" has entered the popular vernacular, Humphrey Bogart (playing Rick Blaine) didn't quite say it that way in the 1941 classic *Casablanca*. What he did say to his piano-playing pal was: **"You played it for her, you can play it for me!"** And when Sam tried to dodge it, Rick added, "If she can stand it, I can. Play it!" Ingrid Bergman, the "she" he is referring to, actually came closer to the misquote earlier in the film by saying, **"Play it, Sam."**

> **Rick: You know what I want to hear.**
>
> **Sam: No, I don't.**
>
> **Rick: You played it for her, you can play it for me!**
>
> **Sam: Well, I don't think I can remember....**
>
> **Rick: If she can stand it, I can! Play it!**

"Life is far too important to be taken seriously."

—*Lord Darlington*

One of the stage's leading wits didn't always boil his quotes down to their minimal states. In this case, what Oscar Wilde's character actually says, in the play *Lady Windermere's Fan*, is as follows: **"Life is far too important a thing ever to talk seriously about it."**

"Gild the lily."

—William Shakespeare

Just one of many phrases Shakespeare introduced to the world via his plays, "gild the lily" has come to mean to dress up something that doesn't need dressing up. The quote, though, has been dressed down from the original. In his play *King John*, Shakespeare wrote: **"To gild refined gold, to paint the lily, to throw a perfume on the violet, to smooth the ice, or add another hue unto the rainbow, or with taper-light to seek the beauteous eye of heaven to garnish, is wasteful and ridiculous excess."**

"I am become death, the destroyer of worlds."

—*The Bhagavad Gita*

These words became part of America history when J. Robert Oppenheimer, director of the Los Alamos laboratory, opted to quote Hindu scripture. But the lines actually read, **"I am all-powerful Time which destroys all things, and I have come here to slay these men."**

"We are not amused."

—*Queen Victoria*

Few (are there any other?) members of a royal family develop a catchphrase. But if you believe all the anecdotal accounts of times when Queen Victoria said this, then she sprouted it more often than boxing announcer Michael Buffer has hollered, **"Let's get ready to Ruuuummmmmble!"** According to *RadioTimes*, though, the Queen may never have said it. And that's backed up by her granddaughter, Princess Alice, who said in an interview: "I asked her, and she never said it." Muddying the waters further, after seeing a production of *Othello*, Queen Victoria noted in her diary, **"I was very much amused indeed!"**

"A penny saved is a penny earned."

—Ben Franklin

Although the Founding Father is credited with the phrase, it's actually not one of his—nor does it belong to his pseudonym, **Poor Richard**.

A version of it—**"A penny spar'd is twice get"**— goes back to about 1633, when it appeared in print for what is believed to be the first time in George Herbert's "Outlandish Proverbs." Another variation popped up in 1661 in "The History of the Worthies of England," nearly 50 years before Franklin's birth. The phrase, as we known it now, was included in an 1899 edition of *Pall Mall Magazine*. What about Ben? He did say, "A penny saved is two pence clear; a pin a day's a groat a year." And, later, in *Poor Richard's Almanac*, he wrote, **"A penny saved is a penny got."**

"Nice guys finish last."

—*Leo Durocher*

Baseball manager Durocher, in his autobiography named, of course, *Nice Guys Finish Last*, explained the origin, saying he was watching a rival team enter the field. "Take a look at that Number Four there," he recalled saying, "A nicer guy never drew breath than that man there. I called off his players' names as they came marching up the steps behind him, 'Walker Cooper, Mize, Marshall, Kerr, Gordon, Thomson. Take a look at them. All nice guys. They'll finish last. Nice guys. Finish last.'" Only problem is, that differs from the original newspaper appearance of the quote, which read, **"The nice guys are all over there, in seventh place."** He was also quoted as saying **"Nice guys don't win pennants."**

That ambiguity makes this an appropriate place to finish this book.

INDEX OF NAMES

People to whom quotes are misattributed have their names in bold.

ABOUT THE AUTHOR

Author, journalist, and playwright **Lou Harry** has penned dozens of books, which have collectively sold more than a million-and-a-half copies. He serves as editor of *Quill*, the magazine of the Society of Professional Journalists, hosts the Lou Harry Gets Real podcast, and freelances for a wide range of publications. He lives in Indianapolis. Follow him on Twitter @louharry.

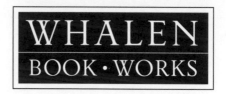

PUBLISHING PRACTICAL & CREATIVE NONFICTION

Whalen Book Works is a small, independent book publishing company based in Kennebunkport, Maine, that combines top-notch design, unique formats, and fresh content to create truly innovative gift books.

Our unconventional approach to bookmaking is a close-knit, creative, and collaborative process among authors, artists, designers, editors, and booksellers. We publish a small, carefully curated list each season, and we take the time to make each book exactly what it needs to be.

We believe in giving back. That's why we plant one tree for every ten books we print. Your purchase supports a tree in the Rocky Mountain National Park.

Visit us at **Whalenbooks.com**
or write to us at
68 North Street, Kennebunkport, ME 04046